KOMODO ISLAND

AND OTHER PLACES RULED BY ANIMALS

TOM JACKSON

Lerner Publications ◆ Minneapolis

Lerner Publications Company
An imprint of Lerner Publishing Group, Inc.
241 First Avenue North
Minneapolis, MN 55401 USA

For reading levels and more information, look up this title at www.lernerbooks.com.

Main body text set in Aptifer Sans LT Pro 14/18.
Typeface provided by Linotype.

Library of Congress Cataloging-in-Publication Data

Names: Jackson, Tom, 1972–author.
Title: Komodo Island and other places ruled by animals / Tom Jackson.
Description: Minneapolis : Lerner Publications, 2024. | Series: Ultimate adventure guides |Includes
    bibliographical references and index. | Audience: Ages 8–11 | Audience: Grades 4–6 |Summary: "From
    reptile islands to monkeys that hang out in volcanic pools, this book is sure to keep you reading.
    Full-color photographs and fun traveler's checklists help bring these amazing places to
    you"—Provided by publisher.
Identifiers: LCCN 2023009278 (print) | LCCN 2023009279 (ebook) | ISBN 9798765609217
    (library binding) | ISBN 9798765625088 (paperback) | ISBN 9798765618745 (epub)
Subjects: LCSH: Habitat selection—Juvenile literature. | Habitat (Ecology)—Juvenile literature.
Classification: LCC QH541.14 .J33 2024 (print) | LCC QH541.14 (ebook) | DDC 577—dc23/eng/20230612

LC record available at https://lccn.loc.gov/2023009278
LC ebook record available at https://lccn.loc.gov/2023009279

Manufactured in the United States of America
1 – CG – 12/15/23

Table of Contents

Chapter 1

LAND OF REPTILES

Sailors of old wrote on their maps "Here Be Dragons!" to show where they had seen terrifying monsters. These words do not appear on today's maps, but there are places in the world that are still ruled by real-life dragons and other fascinating reptiles.

Komodo Island, Indonesia

Dragons live on Komodo. Along with a few smaller islands nearby, this is the home of the world's largest lizard, known as the Komodo dragon. This monster is 10 feet (3 m) from nose to tail and weighs 330 pounds (150 kg).

The lizard lies in wait among the palm trees and tall grass, and then rushes out to grab hold of its victim with long hooked claws. The lizard has a venomous bite. The poison can takes hours, sometimes days, to kill big prey.

The lizard is the biggest and meanest hunter around. Most often it attacks wild pigs, but the dragons will also eat each other.

Snake Island, Brazil

Ilha de Queimada Grande, a rugged island off southern Brazil, has another name: Snake Island. No one lives here, and few humans dare visit because it is ruled by golden lancehead vipers, one of the rarest and deadliest snakes in the world. A bite from one snake would kill a person in less than an hour, and there are about 3,000 vipers on the tiny island.

Golden lanceheads only live wild on Snake Island.

Snake Island is covered in thick forest, and there are few animals for the hungry vipers to eat down on the ground. So the snakes slither onto tree branches where they wait for birds to take a rest during a flight across the ocean. The snake's powerful venom kills the little birds in seconds. There is no escape from Snake Island.

The snakes grow to about 3 feet (91 cm) long.

Traveler's Checklist ✓

✓ **Get permission.** The island is run by Brazil's navy and normally only scientists are allowed to visit.

✓ **Wear sturdy boots, long pants and shirts.** The island is very rocky and has thick, tangled forests that will scratch your skin.

Galápagos Islands, Ecuador

Not every reptile is a terrifying killer. The biggest creatures on the Galápagos Islands, far out in the Pacific Ocean, are giant tortoises. An adult is about 4 feet (1.2 m) long and weighs 700 pounds (320 kg), which is almost as much as a horse! But giant tortoises are slower than a horse with a top speed of just 0.16 miles per hour (0.25 km/h).

Tortoises with domed shells live on mountainous rainy islands and eat lush grass.

The tortoises on lower, drier islands eat the leaves of spindly shrubs and have saddle-shaped shells that let the reptiles stretch their neck upward to reach food.

Chapter 2

MAMMALS RULE!

It could be said that the whole world is ruled by mammals. Mammals can live just about anywhere from hot deserts to icy mountaintops—and far out to sea. However, there are some standout places where mammals really make their presence felt!

Kodiak Island, Alaska

This island is home to the biggest of the big, the Kodiak bear. This huge hunter is the largest type of grizzly bear in the world. A male bear weighs as much as ten people. When standing on its back legs, it reaches the height of a basketball hoop.

Bears prefer to be left alone and will attack if they feel scared.

The bear could kill any animal it meets, but it spends most days fishing for salmon in the rivers or searching for berries. In the fall, the bear hibernates to avoid the cold winter and doesn't come out until June.

Kodiak Island is a cold mountainous place, covered in thick forests and bushy grasses.

The monkeys spend the day in the warm water and then climb back up into trees to sleep at night.

Jigokudani, Japan

The Japanese name for this remote mountain nature reserve in northern Japan is "Hell Valley." It gets that name from all the hot volcanic pools in the area. However, the gang of snow monkeys that live here find it a very comfortable place. Snow monkeys, also called Japanese macaques, live all over the country.

When the cold winter comes to this part of Japan, the monkeys grow thicker hair and huddle together for warmth. Most are forced to head south where the weather is warmer. However, the snow monkeys of Jigokudani can stay right where they are all winter. They keep warm by taking long baths in the hot springs!

A baby monkey is born in summer and stays close to its mother through its first winter.

Traveler's Checklist ✓

☑ **Take a camera.** The monkeys stay in the pool for hours and are used to having human visitors.

☑ **Wear warm clothes.** The monkeys live here all year but only bathe when the weather is cold.

☑ **Wear comfortable shoes.** You cannot drive to the pools and it is at least a 30-minute walk to the entrance.

BC20983

Ger
★ 25.
DEPAR

MALAYSIA
KLIA 2
25.03.15

DEC

Spain ✈
04/10/16
ARRIVAL

BRAZIL IMMIGRATION
MAR
14
DEPARTURE • DEPARTURE • DEPARTURE
BRAZIL IMMIGRATION

16 Paris ✈ JKE6
OCT France 1355
INTERNATIONAL AIRPORT 3568

✈ USA ✈
IMMIGRATION
16

Ngorongoro Crater, Tanzania

East Africa is famous for its grasslands, or savannas, filled with animals like elephants, giraffes, and zebras. Ngorongoro is a big volcanic crater in the middle of the savanna. Filled with grass, forest, and lakes, this is the perfect home for animals. It is also why there are more lions here than anywhere else on Earth. There are about sixty lions in the crater, living in groups called prides. The prides hunt at night, and the lions eat so much that they snooze all day.

At sunset, the crater lions get hungry and set off to kill again.

WHAT MADE THE CRATER?

Ngorongoro Crater is surrounded by a wall of hills. It is so big that most of Philadelphia could fit inside. Around 2.5 million years ago there was a huge volcano here, one of the tallest in Africa. Once the volcano had finished erupting it created an enormous empty space deep underneath where the lava had been. This chamber collapsed, and the whole mountain fell inside leaving the wide crater in its place.

Chapter 3

BIRD WORLDS

Birds are the explorers of the animal world. There is nowhere that these feathered fliers cannot reach by soaring through the sky. Check out these awesome areas ruled by birds.

South Georgia

This mountainous island is near Antarctica. It is cold most of the time and that is why penguins love it. The beaches are often crowded with king penguins most days. These seabirds gather here in spring to breed. The female lays one big egg. When it hatches both mom and dad take turns looking after the chick.

It takes nearly a year and a half for a king penguin chick to grow up enough to take care of itself. This is because king penguins are one of the world's biggest birds. They grow to 39 inches (100 cm) tall and weigh 40 pounds (18 kg).

The chunky penguin chicks have a warm coat of fluffy feathers. The black and white adults have sleek, waterproof feathers.

The baby bird is still not fully grown once winter arrives. The parents must leave the chicks on the beach and head out to sea to hunt. It will be months before their parents come back with more food, and the chicks survive thanks to a layer of fat under their skin. During their second summer, the chicks shed their baby feathers and grow a sleek adult coat. These penguins are ready for their first swim!

The chick eats bits of fish and squid brought up from its parent's stomach.

Lake Natron, Kenya

This shallow lake is in a dry part of East Africa. Its water is filled with poisonous minerals that would burn your skin if you went for a paddle. However, the lake is filled with thousands of flamingos. These pink birds stand on one leg, swapping feet from time to time, to give their tough skin a break from the water.

The lesser flamingo, easy to spot by its black beak, lives in southern and eastern Africa as well as parts of India.

No plants or animals live in the water. Instead it is a warm soup of germ-like bacteria, and this is what the birds eat. The bacteria have red chemicals in them, and this makes the flamingos pink. When they hatch, flamingo chicks have white feathers. Their mom and dad build a mound of mud for the baby bird to sit on. That keeps the chick out of the chemical-filled water. However, the growing chick will soon be tough enough to paddle around under the watchful eye of the adults.

About 2.5 million flamingos gather at Lake Natron to breed each year.

HOW DO FLAMINGOS EAT?

Flamingos can only eat when their head is upside down. They stoop down with their long neck and slurp food from the water. The bacteria food is too small to bite or chew on, so bird has to filter it out from a mouthful of mud! Inside, the beak has a comb-like sieve that traps the food as the bird swings its mouth from side to side through the murky water.

Chapter 4

JUST PASSING THROUGH

Some animals are always on the move, making a lifelong journey called a migration. During migrations animals can gather in huge numbers, too many to count. These animals take over the areas they pass through, and they'll be back next year.

Christmas Island, Australia

This island is in the Indian Ocean, far to the east of the rest of Australia. It was given its name by explorers visiting on Christmas Day. The island is home to a red crab that lives not in the ocean but in the forests. Each year, the crabs must visit the beach to breed and lay their eggs in the water. Around 30 million crabs make this journey at the same time! They all set off when the rains start in October and it takes about one week for them to reach the coast.

After a few weeks living in the sea, tiny baby crabs turn the beach red as they swarm into the forest. It will take four years for them to reach full, adult size.

Sierra Madre Mountains, Mexico

These mountains in the middle of Mexico have thick forests of oyamel fir trees. Each year, around November, billions of monarch butterflies flutter into these quiet valleys and pick a perch high in the branches. The colorful butterflies have flown south from as far away as the Great Lakes.

The crowds of hibernating butterflies weigh enough to bend the tree's branches.

Traveler's Checklist ☑

☑ **Bring a warm jacket.** The butterflies are here during the coldest part of the year.

☑ **No talking please; noise disturbs the insects.**

☑ **Take some binoculars.** The butterflies are too high up to see closely.

BC20983

Ger ✱ 25.

DEPAR

MALAYSIA
KLIA 2
25.03.15

DEC 16

8

Spain ✈
04/10/16

MAR
14

USA
MMIGRATIO
C 16

JKE6
1355
16 Paris 3568
OCT France
INTERNATIONAL AIRPORT

The insects come here to avoid the icy winters further north, but even here the ground can get frosty. This is why the butterflies hang in the trees waiting for the warm weather to return in February. Then the butterflies head out again, fluttering north. It will take all summer for the grandchildren and great grandchildren of these butterflies to reach Canada. And then it will be time for them to fly back to Mexico!

When spring returns the first thing the butterflies do is sip some water. They have not had a drink for several weeks.

The Sardine Run lasts for three months and so there are plenty of fish for this 10-foot (3 m) copper shark.

Cape of Agulhas, South Africa

The most southern point of Africa is called Cape of Agulhas. It is where a warm ocean current from the Indian Ocean meets with a cold one from the Atlantic. The crash of two oceans causes one of the biggest fish migrations on Earth, known as the Sardine Run. Vast numbers of tiny floating plants and animals called plankton grow in the mixed-up water.

Each winter billions of sardines arrive to eat the plankton. The fish form a shoal that is 5 miles (8 km) long, 1 mile (1.6 km) wide and 100 feet (30 m) deep. It would take 150,000 Olympic swimming pools to hold all the fish! The Sardine Run also attracts swarms of hungry sharks, dolphins, and seabirds, which feast day and night.

WHERE IN THE WORLD?

Kodiak Island, Alaska

NORTH AMERICA

Sierra Madre Mountains, Mexico

Atlantic Ocean

Galápagos Islands, Ecuador

SOUTH AMERICA

Snake Island, Brazil

Pacific Ocean

South Georgia

Arctic Ocean

EUROPE

ASIA

Jigokudani,
Japan

Pacific Ocean

Lake Natron,
Kenya

Ngorongoro Crater,
Tanzania

Christmas Island,
Australia

Komodo Island,
Indonesia

AFRICA

Indian Ocean

AUSTRALIA

Cape of Agulhas,
South Africa

Southern Ocean

Glossary

bacterium: a kind of tiny life-form that lives in all parts of the world; a few types of bacteria cause diseases.

hibernate: when an animal takes a rest period during winter; it does not eat and sleeps for a long time.

mammal: a warm-blooded animal that has hairy skin for at least part of its life, and whose young feed on its mother's milk

microscopic: too small to see without a microscope, a very powerful kind of magnifier

migration: when animals make a long, round-trip journey to find new places to feed and breed

mineral: a natural chemical found in soil, rocks, and water

plankton: tiny life-forms that float in water

reptile: an animal covered in scales; reptiles include snakes, turtles, and lizards

shoal: a group of fish or other sea creatures.

venomous: using poison as a weapon in hunting and defense

volcanic: having to do with volcanoes

Learn More

BBC Bitesize: Let's Explore the Galápagos Islands
https://bbc.co.uk/bitesize/topics/z3fycdm/
articles/zk9cxyc

Hobbie, Ann. *Monarch Butterflies*. North Adams, MA: Storey
Publishing, 2021.

Markle, Sandra. *On the Hunt with Grizzly Bears*. Minneapolis:
Lerner Publications, 2023.

National Geographic Kids: Komodo Dragon
https://kids.nationalgeographic.com/animals/reptiles/
facts/komodo-dragon

Parks Australia: Red Crab Migration
https://parksaustralia.gov.au/christmas/discover/
highlights/red-crab-migration

Riggs, Kate. *Flamingos*. Mankato, MN: The Creative
Company, 2023.

Index

Photo Acknowledgments

Image credits: Tetyana Dotsenko/Shutterstock.com, p. 1; Sergey Uryadnikov/Shutterstock.com, p. 5; Minden Pictures/Alamy Stock Photo, p. 6a; Xico Putini/Shutterstock.com, p. 6b; Nayeryouakim/ Wikimedia Commons, p. 7a; Lars Poyansky/Shutterstock.com, pp. 7b, 13b, 24b; happpy.designer/ Shutterstock.com, p. 7c; MarijaPiliponyte, p. 7d; Danita Delimont/Shutterstock.com, p. 8; Fotogrin/ Shutterstock.com, p. 9; bobby20/Shutterstock.com, p. 11a; slowmotiongli/Shutterstock.com, p. 11b; BlueOrange Studio/Shutterstock.com, p. 12; gu3ree/Shutterstock.com, p. 13a; olllikeballoon/ Shutterstock.com, pp. 13c, 24d; Mochipet/Shutterstock.com, p. 13d; Travel Stock/Shutterstock.com, p. 14a; Adalbert Dragon/Shutterstock.com, p. 14b; Jen Watson/Shutterstock.com, p. 15; Zaruba Ondrej/ Shutterstock.com, p. 17; Zaruba Ondrej/Shutterstock.com, p. 18; Cucumber Images/Shutterstock.com, p. 19; Danita Delimont/Shutterstock.com, p. 20; Carl Nelson/Shutterstock.com, p. 23a; Sascha Caballero/ Shutterstock.com, p. 23b; Photo Spirit/Shutterstock.com, p. 24a; wenchiawang/Shutterstock.com, p. 24c; Noradoa/Shutterstock.com, p. 25; wildestanimal/Shutterstock.com, p. 26-27; Andrei Minsk/Shutterstock. com, p. 28-29; Cover: Sergey Uryadnikov/Shutterstock.com.